Navigating Property Co-Ownership in Florida:

A Comprehensive Guide to Partition Actions and Heirs Property Law

Matthew E. Mazur, Jr., Esq.

Special Thanks To My Editor

I am deeply thankful to Sahr O. Dumbar, Esq. for his invaluable guidance and support throughout the writing of this book. His attention to detail and commitment to excellence have greatly enhanced its quality. Thank you, Sahr for your dedication as an editor and for being the best trial co-counsel in Florida.

Contents

Introduction

Navigating the complexities of shared property ownership in Florida can often feel like walking through a maze without a map. The emotional, financial, and legal challenges that accompany co-ownership disputes are not just obstacles; they are genuine pain points that can strain relationships, drain resources, and cloud the future of your property. Whether it's a family home steeped in memories, an investment property bought with hard-earned money, or land inherited from loved ones, the stakes are invariably high, and the path to resolution can seem daunting.

The Challenge of Shared Property Ownership

Shared property ownership, while offering numerous benefits, can become a source of significant stress and conflict. The reasons are manifold: disagreements over property management, divergent visions for the property's future, financial pressures, and, in the case of inherited property, the emotional weight of familial expectations and legacies. These challenges are compounded by the legal complexities of property law in Florida, making it difficult for co-owners to find common ground, much less navigate the intricacies of resolving their disputes.

Overview of Partition Actions and Heirs Property Law in Florida

At the heart of resolving co-ownership disputes in Florida are Partition Actions under (Florida Statutes Chapter 64, Part I (64.011-64.091)) and the Uniform Partition of Heirs Property Act (Florida Statutes Chapter 64, Part II (64.201-64.214)). Partition Actions provide a legal avenue for co-owners to address and resolve their differences, either through the division of the property (if feasible) or its sale, with proceeds distributed among the owners according to their shares. This process is designed to ensure fairness and equity, offering a structured resolution that courts can oversee.

The Heirs Property Law, a relatively recent addition to Florida's legal landscape, specifically addresses the unique challenges of inherited property. Recognizing the complexities and emotional ties that often accompany heirs' property, this law offers protections and considerations to prevent the loss of family land and ensure that any partition action respects the heritage and intentions of the original owners. It's a significant step towards balancing the scales in partition actions, providing a more nuanced approach to disputes that involve deeply personal and familial dimensions.

How This Guide Can Help You

This guide is crafted with the understanding that behind every co-ownership dispute lies a web of personal stories, aspirations, and concerns. Our aim is to untangle this web, offering clarity and direction through the maze of legal procedures and emotional challenges. By focusing on the pain points of potential clients, we provide not just educational information but also practical solutions and strategies to navigate the complexities of Partition Actions and Heirs Property Law in Florida.

We delve into the nuances of these laws, breaking down legal jargon into understandable language, and highlighting key considerations that can influence the outcome of your case. From understanding your rights and obligations as a co-owner to exploring the strategic advantages of partition actions and the protective measures offered by the Heirs Property Law, this guide is designed to empower you with knowledge and confidence.

Whether you're at the beginning of your journey, feeling overwhelmed by the prospect of legal action, or you're seeking a way to protect your property and your relationships, this guide is your compass. It's a resource to help you understand your options, make informed decisions, and ultimately, find a path to resolution that honors your interests and those of your co-owners. In the following sections, we'll explore the intricacies of Partition Actions and Heirs Property Law in detail, offering insights, advice, and real-world strategies to navigate these challenges effectively. Our goal is to transform what may seem like insurmountable obstacles into manageable steps towards a solution, ensuring that you're not just prepared to face the challenges of shared property ownership but equipped to overcome them.

Chapter I:

Understanding Your Pain Points

Navigating the turbulent waters of property co-ownership in Florida can be both emotionally draining and financially taxing. The journey is often fraught with conflicts that extend beyond the mere division of property, touching the very core of personal relationships and financial stability. In this section, we delve into the pain points that you, as a co-owner, might be experiencing, focusing on the emotional and financial toll of property disputes, as well as the unique complexities that come with managing inherited property.

The Emotional and Financial Toll of Property Disputes

Emotional Stress of Co-Ownership Conflicts

The emotional impact of disputes over shared property cannot be overstated. For many, a property is not just a physical asset but a repository of memories and emotions. When disagreements arise— whether over its use, management, or sale—the stress can strain or even sever the bonds between family members, friends, or investment partners. The constant tension, the endless arguments, and the uncertainty of resolution can lead to sleepless nights and strained days, affecting your mental health and overall well-being.

Financial Implications of Unresolved Property Disputes

Beyond the emotional strain, unresolved property disputes carry significant financial implications. Legal fees can accumulate quickly, turning what might have been a manageable situation into a financial burden. Additionally, the inability to agree on the property's use or sale can lead to missed opportunities for income or investment growth, effectively locking up your financial resources in an asset you cannot leverage. The longer these disputes remain unresolved, the greater the risk of diminishing the property's value, either through neglect or because of an inability to invest in necessary maintenance and improvements.

The Complexity of Inherited Property

Challenges of Managing Heirs' Property

Inherited property, or heirs' property, introduces another layer of complexity to co-ownership disputes. These properties often come to the heirs as a legacy, carrying with them the emotional weight of family history and expectations. Managing such properties can be challenging, especially when there are multiple heirs with differing visions for the property's future. The sentimental value attached to the property can make negotiations and compromises more difficult, as decisions are not just about financial gain but about honoring and preserving a family legacy.

The Impact of Not Having a Clear Legal Path

One of the most significant pain points in dealing with inherited property is the lack of a clear legal path for resolution when the ownership of the property does not specify percentages of ownership among the heirs. With or without a will, or estate plan in place, the property falls into a legal gray area, governed by state laws that may not reflect the wishes of the deceased or the best interests of the heirs. This can lead to protracted legal battles, further draining emotional and financial resources. The introduction of the Heirs Property Law in Florida was a step toward addressing this issue, providing a framework for resolving disputes over inherited property in a way that considers both the financial and emotional stakes involved.

Understanding these pain points is the first step toward finding a resolution. The emotional and financial toll of property disputes, compounded by the complexities of managing inherited property, can seem overwhelming. However, with the right information and guidance, it is possible to navigate these challenges effectively. In the following sections, we will explore the legal mechanisms available to you, including Partition Actions and the Heirs Property Law, offering strategies to address, and overcome these pain points, and move toward a resolution that honors both your financial interests and your emotional connections to the property.

Chapter II:

Partition Actions – Your Path to Resolution

In the labyrinth of property co-ownership disputes, Partition Actions emerge as a beacon of hope, offering a structured path to resolution that balances the scales of justice and fairness. This section delves into the essence of Partition Actions, exploring their definition, types, and the process of filing, while highlighting the indispensable role of legal representation in navigating these waters.

What is a Partition Action?

Definition and Purpose

A Partition Action is a legal procedure used to resolve disputes among co-owners of real property. When co-owners cannot agree on the use, management, or sale of their property, a Partition Action allows them to seek a court-ordered division or sale of the property. The purpose of this action is to ensure that each co-owner's investment and interest in the property are fairly recognized and compensated, providing a clear, equitable path out of co-ownership conflicts.

How It Offers a Solution to Co-Ownership Disputes

Partition Actions address the core issues of co-ownership disputes by removing the deadlock that prevents property from being used or sold to its best potential. Whether it results in a physical division of the property (partition in kind) or a sale and division of proceeds (partition by sale), it offers a definitive resolution that respects the rights and interests of all parties involved. This legal avenue ensures that no co-owner is left at a disadvantage, providing a fair and impartial solution to often emotionally charged disputes.

Types of Partition Actions in Florida

Partition by Sale

In cases where the property cannot be equitably divided (due to its nature or because division would significantly diminish its value), the court may order a partition by sale. This involves selling the property on the open market or through an auction and dividing the proceeds among the co-owners according to their respective shares minus any attorney's fees and costs owed. This type is often seen as a last resort but can be the most practical solution for properties that do not lend themselves to physical division.

Partition in Kind

A partition in kind, or physical division of the property, is preferred when it's possible to divide the property without diminishing its overall value. This allows co-owners to retain their tangible share of the property, which can be particularly important for large tracts of land or when co-owners have a strong attachment to the physical property. However, this type of partition is less common due to the complexities involved in dividing property equitably.

Considerations for Choosing the Right Type

Choosing between a partition by sale and a partition in kind depends on several factors, including the nature of the property, the relationship between co-owners, and their long-term goals. Financial considerations, potential tax implications, and the sentimental value of the property also play crucial roles in this decision. Understanding the advantages and limitations of each type is essential for co-owners to make informed decisions that align with their interests and objectives.

The Process of Filing a Partition Action

Step-by-Step Guide from Filing to Resolution

1. **Filing the Petition**: The process begins with one or more co-owners filing a petition for partition in the relevant court,

detailing the property in question, the ownership shares, and the desired type of partition.

2. **Service of Process**: The petition must be served to all other co-owners, notifying them of the action and giving them an opportunity to respond.

3. **Appointment of a Special Master**: The court may appoint a special master to oversee the partition process, assess the property, and recommend the best course of action to the court.

4. **Valuation and Division**: The property is appraised to determine its fair market value. This valuation allows for a determination to be made as to whether one co-owner can buy out the other co-owner. In the event that a buy out is not feasible the valuation, allows the court to make a determination as to whether a partition in kind is feasible or if a sale is necessary.

5. **Distribution of Proceeds or Property**: Finally, the proceeds from a sale or the divided property are distributed among the co-owners according to their shares.

Legal Requirements and Documentation

The legal requirements for filing a Partition Action include a clear description of the property, evidence of ownership, and the specific shares of each co-owner. Documentation may include deeds, titles, and any agreements related to the property's ownership and use. Ensuring accuracy and completeness in this documentation is crucial for a smooth process.

The Role of Legal Representation

Why Legal Guidance is Crucial

Navigating the complexities of Partition Actions requires not just an understanding of the law but an ability to strategize and advocate for your best interests. Legal guidance ensures that your case is presented compellingly and that all procedural requirements are met. An attorney who understands heirs' property and partitions can also negotiate on your behalf, potentially reaching a resolution that avoids the need for a court-ordered partition.

How to Choose the Right Attorney for Your Case

Choosing the right attorney involves considering their experience with Partition Actions and their approach to client representation. Look for an attorney who communicates clearly, understands your objectives, and demonstrates a commitment to achieving the best possible outcome for your case. Personal referrals and initial consultations can be valuable resources in making this important decision.

Understanding the nuances of this legal process and enlisting the right legal help are critical steps toward achieving a fair and equitable resolution.

Chapter III:

The Heirs Property Act – Protecting Your Legacy

In the realm of property co-ownership, inherited property stands out as a unique and emotionally charged issue. The Heirs Property Act in Florida represents a significant advancement in the way the legal system addresses the complexities of inherited property, offering a beacon of hope and protection for those looking to safeguard their family's legacy. This section explores the background, benefits, and practical implications of the Heirs Property Act, providing insights into how it can serve as a powerful tool in resolving inherited property disputes.

Understanding the Heirs Property Act

Background and Significance

The Heirs Property Act was enacted to address the specific challenges faced by heirs of property that has been passed down through generations without a clear will or estate plan. This type of property, often referred to as "heirs' property," can become a source of legal disputes and financial vulnerability, particularly when external parties attempt to acquire interests in the property at below-market prices. The Act provides a legal framework that recognizes the unique nature of heirs' property and offers mechanisms to protect the rights and interests of family members.

How It Changes the Game for Inherited Property Disputes

Before the Heirs Property Act, the resolution of disputes over inherited property was often cumbersome and inequitable, leading to forced sales and loss of family land. The Act introduces key provisions that ensure a fair process for partition actions involving heirs' property, including requirements for notice, appraisal, and the option for family members to buy out the interests of co-owners wishing to sell. This shifts the dynamics of inherited property disputes, empowering heirs to retain their property and protect their legacy.

Benefits of the Heirs Property Act for Property Owners

Enhanced Protections for Heirs

One of the most significant benefits of the Heirs Property Act is the enhanced protections it offers to heirs. These protections include the right to receive a formal notice of any partition action, the requirement for a fair market value appraisal by a neutral third party, and the opportunity for family members to purchase the interests of those wishing to sell. These provisions ensure that heirs are not blindsided by legal actions and have a fair chance to maintain ownership of their family property.

Preventing Loss and Ensuring Fair Valuation

The Act plays a crucial role in preventing the loss of family property to investors or developers looking to capitalize on heirs' property disputes. By mandating a fair market value appraisal and providing a mechanism for family buyouts, the Act ensures that any sale of the property reflects its true value, protecting the financial interests of heirs. This is particularly important in communities where property values are rising, safeguarding against the exploitation of heirs' property for below-market prices.

Navigating Partition Actions Under the Heirs Property Act

Specific Considerations and Steps

Navigating partition actions under the Heirs Property Act requires an understanding of the specific provisions and steps involved. Heirs must be proactive in asserting their rights under the Act, from ensuring proper notice and participation in the appraisal process to exploring options for buyouts. It's also crucial to engage with legal representation experienced in heirs' property issues to navigate the complexities of the Act effectively.

By understanding the Act's provisions and leveraging its protections, heirs can navigate partition actions with confidence, ensuring that their family's legacy is preserved for future generations. With the right approach and legal guidance, the challenges of inherited property can be transformed into opportunities for unity, preservation, and growth.

Chapter IV:

Overcoming Common Challenges

The path to resolving property co-ownership disputes is often fraught with obstacles that can seem insurmountable. From co-owner resistance to valuation disputes and concerns about legal costs and timelines, these challenges can exacerbate the stress and uncertainty of an already difficult situation. This section offers practical advice and strategies for overcoming these common hurdles, empowering you to navigate the complexities of partition actions with confidence and clarity.

Dealing with Co-Owner Resistance

Strategies for Negotiation and Mediation

Co-owner resistance is a frequent challenge in partition actions, often rooted in emotional attachments, financial disagreements, or differing visions for the property's future. Effective negotiation and mediation are key to overcoming this resistance. Start by seeking common ground and understanding the underlying concerns driving the resistance. Employing a neutral third-party mediator can facilitate open communication, helping all parties to explore mutually beneficial solutions. Remember, the goal is to reach an agreement that respects everyone's interests and minimizes conflict.

Legal Options When Consensus is Unreachable

When negotiation and mediation fail to break the deadlock, legal options remain to move forward with a partition action. Filing a petition for partition in court can initiate a process that ultimately resolves the dispute through legal means. While this approach may escalate tensions in the short term, it provides a structured path to resolution, ensuring that the rights and interests of all co-owners are fairly considered and adjudicated.

Valuation Disputes and Fair Market Value

Understanding Valuation in Partition Actions

Valuation disputes arise when co-owners disagree on the fair market value of the property, a critical factor in determining the outcome of both partition by sale and partition in kind. Accurate valuation is essential for ensuring that the division of proceeds or property is equitable. It's important to understand that valuation in partition actions involves assessing not just the current market value but also considering factors such as potential use, income generation, and any encumbrances on the property.

How to Ensure a Fair Assessment

To ensure a fair assessment, insist on using a qualified, independent appraiser with experience in the local real estate market and, if possible, in partition actions. Both parties should agree on the choice of appraiser to increase trust in the valuation process. In cases of significant disagreement, each party may choose to hire their own appraiser, and if discrepancies in valuation arise, the court may appoint a third appraiser to conduct an independent evaluation.

Legal Costs and Timelines

Managing Expectations and Planning Financially

Understanding and managing expectations regarding legal costs and timelines are crucial for navigating partition actions. Legal expenses can vary widely based on the complexity of the case, the cooperation (or lack thereof) of all parties, and the need for expert witnesses or appraisals. Be proactive in discussing potential costs with your attorney and plan financially for the possibility of a prolonged legal process. Consider setting aside a reserve fund to cover unexpected expenses.

Tips for Streamlining the Process

Streamlining the partition action process can help minimize legal costs and expedite resolution. Clear communication and documentation are key—ensure that all agreements, negotiations, and court filings are well-documented and accessible. Being responsive to your attorney's requests for information and decision-making can also speed up the process. Additionally, consider alternative dispute resolution methods, such as mediation, which can be more time and cost-efficient than court proceedings.

In conclusion, while the challenges of navigating partition actions and co-ownership disputes can be daunting, understanding the strategies and legal mechanisms available to overcome these obstacles can empower you to move forward with confidence. By approaching negotiations with empathy, insisting on fair valuation practices, and managing legal costs and timelines effectively, you can navigate the complexities of partition actions and achieve a resolution that honors your rights and interests.

Chapter V:

Moving Forward – Your Next Steps

Embarking on a partition action to resolve your property co-ownership disputes is a significant step towards reclaiming your peace of mind and securing your financial future. This journey, while complex, can be navigated successfully with careful preparation, the right support team, and a commitment to staying informed and empowered. Here, we outline the essential steps and considerations to help you move forward with confidence.

Preparing for a Partition Action

Gathering Necessary Documents and Information

The foundation of a successful partition action is a thorough and organized collection of all necessary documents and information. This includes the deed to the property, any co-ownership agreements, records of financial contributions to the property (such as mortgage payments, maintenance, and improvements), and any previous correspondence regarding the dispute. Having these documents at hand will not only streamline the legal process but also strengthen your position.

Building Your Support Team: Legal, Financial, and Emotional

A strong support team is invaluable as you navigate the complexities of a partition action. This team should include:

- **Legal**: An experienced attorney who understands partition actions and heirs' property actions in Florida can guide you through the legal landscape, advocate on your behalf, and help you achieve a fair resolution.

- **Financial**: A financial advisor can help you understand the implications of the partition action on your finances and plan for your future.

- **Emotional**: The emotional toll of property disputes cannot be underestimated. Support from friends, family, or a professional counselor can provide the resilience and perspective needed during challenging times.

Choosing the Right Legal Partner

What to Look for in a Partition Attorney

Selecting the right attorney is crucial to the success of your partition action. Look for a legal partner with:

- **Experience**: An attorney with a track record in handling partition actions and a deep understanding of partition law, Heir's property law and real estate law in Florida.

- **Communication**: Someone who communicates clearly and keeps you informed at every step of the process.

- **Empathy**: A legal partner who understands the emotional dimensions of your dispute and approaches your case with sensitivity.

Questions to Ask Potential Legal Representatives

When meeting with potential attorneys, consider asking the following questions to assess their suitability:

- Can you share examples of similar partition actions you have handled?

- How do you approach negotiation and mediation in co-ownership disputes?

- What are your fees, and how are they structured?

- What is your assessment of my case, and how do you foresee it proceeding?

Staying Informed and Empowered

Resources for Further Education

Knowledge is power, especially when navigating legal disputes. Seek out resources that can help you understand the nuances of partition actions and property law in Florida. This might include legal guides, online forums, and workshops or seminars offered by legal aid organizations or real estate associations.

Building a Community of Support

Remember, you're not alone. Many others have navigated similar disputes and can offer valuable insights and encouragement. Look for online communities, support groups, or local meetups of individuals facing co-ownership challenges. Sharing experiences and strategies can provide not only practical advice but also a sense of solidarity.

Moving forward with a partition action is a decisive step towards resolving your property dispute and safeguarding your interests. By preparing thoroughly, choosing the right legal partner, and committing to staying informed and supported, you can navigate this journey with confidence and clarity. Remember, the goal is not just to resolve the dispute, but to emerge from the process empowered and ready for the next chapter of your life.

Conclusion

Navigating the complexities of property co-ownership disputes can be a daunting journey, fraught with emotional and financial challenges. Yet, the path to resolution, illuminated by the mechanisms of Partition Actions and the protections offered by the Heirs Property Act, provides a clear and equitable way forward. These legal avenues are not just about resolving disputes; they're about restoring peace, safeguarding legacies, and opening new opportunities for growth and stability.

Partition Actions offer a structured, fair process for addressing co-ownership conflicts, whether through division or sale of the property, ensuring that each party's interests are recognized and compensated. The Heirs Property Act, on the other hand, provides a critical safety net for inherited property, protecting families from exploitation and loss while honoring the emotional and historical significance of family legacies.

As you stand at the crossroads, contemplating the next steps in your co-ownership dispute, remember that the journey ahead, while challenging, leads to resolution and renewal. The first step, often the hardest, is within your reach. Armed with knowledge, the right support, and legal guidance, you can navigate this path with confidence.

We invite you to take that first step towards resolution. Reach out for a consultation, where we can discuss your situation in detail, explore your options, and outline a strategy tailored to your needs and goals. Together, we can turn the page on disputes and step into a future of clarity and peace.

Appendix: Additional Resources

Glossary of Terms

- **Partition Action**: A legal process to divide jointly owned property among the co-owners or sell it and distribute the proceeds according to each owner's share.

- **Heirs Property**: Heirs property is when a family owns land or a house and passes it down from one generation to the next without officially handling it through a court or legal process. This may mean there is no official paper to clearly show who owns the property or what percentage the heirs own. The result is property that has shared ownership among heirs. There may be situations that impact whether a property is Heirs Property under Florida Statutes.

- **Partition by Sale**: A court-ordered sale of the property, with proceeds divided among co-owners.

- **Partition in Kind**: A physical division of the property, allocating portions to each co-owner.

- **Fair Market Value**: The estimated market value of a property based on current market conditions.

- **Co-Ownership:** Joint ownership of property by two or more parties where each party has an undivided interest in the whole property.

- **Joint Tenancy:** A form of co-ownership where each party owns an equal share of the property, with rights of survivorship.

- **Tenancy in Common:** A form of co-ownership where each party may own a different share of the property, without rights of survivorship.

- **Special Master:** A neutral third party appointed by the court to oversee certain aspects of a legal case, such as the partition process.

- **Legal Standing:** The right of an individual to bring a lawsuit, based on their stake in the outcome of the dispute.

- **Probate:** The legal process through which a deceased person's estate is properly distributed to heirs and designated beneficiaries and any debt owed to creditors is paid off. If a property was a deceased person's homestead, it does not necessarily have to go through Probate.

- **Appraisal:** A professional assessment of a property's value conducted by a certified appraiser.

- **Buyout:** An option in a partition action where one or more co-owners purchase the interest of other co-owner(s) to avoid the sale or division of the property.

- **Equitable Distribution**: The fair and just division of property between co-owners, considering each party's contributions and interests.

- **Rights of Survivorship**: A feature of joint tenancy where, upon the death of one co-owner, their interest in the property automatically passes to the surviving co-owner(s), bypassing the probate process.

- **Market Trends**: General movements in the real estate market that affect property values, including factors like supply and demand, economic conditions, and interest rates.

- **Certified Appraiser**: A professional who has received certification to conduct property appraisals, ensuring an unbiased and accurate assessment of property value.

- **Buyout Agreement**: A legal agreement where one or more co-owners agree to purchase another co-owner's share of the property, often used to resolve disputes without resorting to a partition by sale.

- **Litigation**: The process of taking legal action in court to resolve disputes, including partition actions.

- **Mediation**: A form of alternative dispute resolution where a neutral third party (mediator) helps co-owners negotiate a mutually acceptable solution to their dispute.

- **Clear Title:** Legal documentation proving a property owner's right to sell the property, free of liens or other encumbrances.

- **Encumbrance:** A claim, lien, charge, or liability attached to and binding real property that may lessen its value or obstruct the use of the property.

- **Equitable Distribution:** The fair division of property between co-owners based on their respective interests and expenses related to the property.

- **Forced Sale:** A court-ordered sale of property, typically in the context of a Partition Action, where the property is sold against the wishes of one or more co-owners.

- **Heir:** A person legally entitled to inherit property from a deceased individual's estate under the laws of intestacy or under the terms of a will.

- **Intestate:** The condition of dying without a valid will, resulting in the deceased's estate being distributed according to state laws of intestacy.

- **Lien:** A legal right or interest that a creditor has in the debtor's property, typically lasting until the debt that it secures is paid.

Title Search: A process conducted to determine the legal ownership of property and identify any encumbrances or liens before a sale or transfer.

FAQ about Partition Actions and Heirs Property Law

Q: Can a Partition Action be avoided? A: Yes, if co-owners can reach an agreement through negotiation or mediation, a partition action can be avoided. Legal guidance can help explore these alternatives.

Q: How is the fair market value of the property determined in a Partition Action? A: The court typically orders an appraisal by a neutral third party to determine the fair market value, considering current market conditions and the property's characteristics.

Q: What protections does the Heirs Property Act offer? A: The Act provides protections such as requiring a fair market value appraisal, offering buyout options to family members, and ensuring all heirs are properly notified of legal actions.

Q: How long does a Partition Action take? A: The timeline can vary significantly based on the complexity of the case, the property's characteristics, and the court's schedule. Your attorney can provide a more specific estimate based on your situation.

Q: How can I choose the right attorney for my Partition Action? A: Look for an attorney with experience in real estate and partition actions, a track record of successful resolutions, and who communicates clearly and empathetically. Don't hesitate to ask potential attorneys about their experience and approach to similar cases.

Embarking on a Partition Action or navigating the Heirs Property Act may seem overwhelming, but with the right information and support, you can achieve a fair and equitable resolution to your property dispute. Remember, the first step towards peace and clarity is within reach.

Q: What happens if co-owners cannot agree on whether to sell or keep the property? A: If co-owners cannot reach an agreement, any co-owner can file a Partition Action, asking the court to intervene and decide on the property's fate—whether it should be sold or divided. The court's decision will be based on what is deemed most fair and equitable to all parties involved.

Q: Are all co-owners entitled to an equal share of the proceeds in a Partition by Sale? A: Not necessarily. The distribution of proceeds from a sale in a Partition Action is based on each co-owner's ownership interest, which may not always be equal. Contributions to the property's purchase price, payment of property expenses, and improvements made can also affect each co-owner's share.

Q: Can an heir be forced out of their inherited property through a Partition Action? A: Yes, it is possible. If the court orders a partition by sale, the property will be sold, and the proceeds distributed among the heirs. However, the Heirs Property Act provides mechanisms intended to protect heirs from losing their property unfairly, including options for buyouts and considerations for fair market value appraisals.

Q: How can heirs protect their rights under the Heirs Property Act? A: Heirs can protect their rights by ensuring they are properly identified and notified of any legal actions concerning the property, participating in the appraisal process, and exploring buyout options if they wish to retain the property. Consulting with an attorney experienced in heirs' property law is also crucial. If a Partition Action is pending, it is very important that the Affirmative Defense of Heirs Property Act be raised or it can be waived.

Q: What is the difference between a partition in kind and a partition by sale, and how is the type decided? A: A partition in kind involves physically dividing the property among the co-owners, while a partition by sale involves selling the property and dividing the proceeds. The decision on which type to pursue depends on whether the property can be divided without diminishing its value (suitable for partition in kind) or not (leading to a partition by sale). The court will consider the co-owners' preferences, the property's characteristics, and what is most equitable.

Q: Can a Partition Action be stopped once it has started? A: Yes, a Partition Action can be stopped if all co-owners reach an agreement on how to resolve their dispute outside of court. This could involve one or more co-owners buying out the others, agreeing to sell the property and splitting the proceeds, or finding another compromise.

Q: How does the court decide if a property should be divided or sold in a Partition Action? A: The court considers several factors, including the nature of the property, the feasibility of dividing it without diminishing its value, and the preferences of the co-owners. If the property cannot be divided fairly and equitably, or if division would significantly reduce its value, the court may order a sale.

Q: What if one co-owner has invested more in the property than others? A: The court can consider the contributions of each co-owner towards the purchase price, maintenance, improvements, and expenses when determining how to divide the sale proceeds or property. Co-owners who have contributed more may receive a larger share to reflect their investment.

Q: What are the risks of not resolving a co-ownership dispute through a Partition Action? A: Unresolved disputes can lead to ongoing legal and personal conflicts, financial strain from legal costs, and the potential for the property to lose value due to neglect or mismanagement. A Partition Action provides a clear path to resolving these disputes and allows co-owners to move forward.

Q: How can co-owners avoid a Partition Action? A: Co-owners can avoid a Partition Action by negotiating an agreement outside of court, possibly with the help of mediation. This could involve one co-owner buying out the others, agreeing to sell the property and divide the proceeds, or finding another compromise that satisfies all parties.

Q: What should co-owners do if they want to keep the property in the family but cannot agree on its use? A: Co-owners who wish to keep the property in the family but face disagreements on its use should consider mediation to explore creative solutions that meet everyone's needs. Establishing a formal co-ownership agreement that outlines the use, management, and future plans for the property can also prevent disputes.

Q: What if an heir wants to keep the family property but cannot afford to buy out the other heirs? A: In some cases, financial arrangements or loans may be available to heirs wishing to retain the property. Additionally, under the Heirs Property Act, there may be provisions that allow for more favorable buyout options. Depending upon the relationship between the heirs payment plans may be able to be negotiated. Consulting with a legal expert can provide tailored solutions based on the specific circumstances.

Q: How does the presence of a lien affect a Partition Action? A: Liens on the property must be addressed as part of the partition process. The proceeds from a partition by sale are typically used first to satisfy any liens or encumbrances before distributing the remaining funds among the co-owners according to their shares. This ensures that the property is sold with a clear title.

Q: Can an heir be disinherited from receiving a share of an inherited property? A: Generally, an heir can only be disinherited through a will that explicitly excludes them. In the absence of a will (intestate succession), state laws determine the distribution of the deceased's estate among legal heirs. However, specific circumstances and state laws can vary, so it's essential to consult with an attorney for advice related to individual cases.

Q: What role does a title search play in a Partition Action? A: A title search is crucial in a Partition Action to ensure that all legal owners are identified and that any liens, encumbrances, or other legal issues are addressed before the division or sale of the property. It helps prevent future disputes and ensures a fair and lawful resolution.

Q: How can heirs prepare for a potential Partition Action? A: Heirs can prepare by gathering all relevant documents related to the property, including deeds, wills, and records of financial contributions. It's also advisable to discuss intentions and explore potential agreements among heirs before legal action becomes necessary. Engaging with an attorney experienced in heirs' property and partition actions early in the process can provide strategic guidance and help avoid litigation.

Q: Are there alternatives to Partition Actions for resolving disputes over inherited property? A: Yes, alternatives such as mediation or family agreements can be explored to resolve disputes amicably without resorting to court. These alternatives allow heirs to maintain control over the outcome and potentially preserve family relationships while finding a fair solution to property division.

Q: Who is responsible for paying the attorney's fees in a Partition Action? A: Generally, attorney's fees in a Partition Action can be paid in several ways, depending on the case specifics and the court's decision. Often, the fees are paid upfront by the party bringing the partition action. If the partition results in a sale the court may order that those fees be shared by the co-owners in proportion to their ownership interests in the property.

Q: Can attorney's fees be paid upfront by one party? A: Yes, one party may choose to pay attorney's fees upfront, especially if they are initiating the Partition Action. However, they can request reimbursement for a portion of these fees from the other co-owners or from the sale proceeds, subject to the court's approval and based on equitable considerations. These attorney's fees would be prorated based upon the co-owner's interest in the property.

Q: Are attorney's fees determined by the court in a Partition Action? A: In some cases, the court may determine the reasonableness of attorney's fees and decide how they should be allocated among the parties. This is particularly true if there is a dispute over the fees or if the fees are to be paid from the sale proceeds.

Q: What factors influence the amount of attorney's fees in a Partition Action? A: Several factors can influence the amount of attorney's fees, including the complexity of the case, the amount of work required, the property's value, and the attorney's experience and rates. The specific arrangements between the attorney and the client (such as hourly rates, flat fees, or contingency fees) also play a role.

Q: Can attorney's fees be included in the costs of the Partition Action? A: Yes, attorney's fees are often considered part of the costs of the Partition Action, along with other expenses like appraisal fees, court costs, and the costs associated with selling the property (if applicable). These costs are typically deducted from the sale proceeds before distribution to the co-owners or allocated among the co-owners as the court sees fit.

Q: Is it possible to negotiate a payment plan for attorney's fees? A: Yes. Many attorneys are open to negotiating a payment plan for their fees based on the case's specifics and the client's financial situation. It's important to have a clear agreement on fees, payment plans and payment expectations before proceeding with legal representation.

Q: What happens if a co-owner cannot afford to pay their share of the attorney's fees? A: If a co-owner cannot afford to pay their share of the attorney's fees, this issue should be addressed as early as possible. Solutions may include negotiating payment plans and seeking a different arrangement for fee allocation.

About our Firm

We Don't Take Every Case That Comes Through The Door!

This means we have more time for your case. Our firm is not your typical law firm; we don't take every case that comes through the door. We don't rely on a high volume of cases generated by gigantic television, radio, and Yellow Page advertising. We do not claim to handle every type of law under the sun. Quite frankly, we do not want to handle every type of law under the sun because we do not need to.

We are not a television law firm mill. Every year, we accept a limited number of partition and heirs' property cases from the people who ask us to represent them. By not taking every case we have more time for your case, and we believe this gives us the ability to achieve better results overall.

Sometime the best advice you can get when you are contemplating filing a lawsuit is that you do not have a claim that can be won. If after reviewing your case, we find this to be true, we will tell you. However, if after we review you case and we decide to accept it, you can be assured that you will receive the personal attention you.

deserve. We will represent you aggressively, keep you up to date on what is happening in your case, and give you advice as to whether you should settle your case or go to trial.

If you would like more information, visit our website at www.mazurlaw.com. On our website you will find additional useful information on partition actions and heirs' property. If you would like to speak to our firm, please feel free to call us at (305) 466 – 3328 or e-mail us at info@mazur-law.com.

We will explain all the fees and costs to you fully before we start working on your case. Together, as a team, we will decide on the best tactics for your case.

Matthew E. Mazur, Jr., Esq.

Weston,   Florida

www.ingramcontent.com/pod-product-compliance
Lightning Source LLC
Chambersburg PA
CBHW071016290526
45795CB00005B/1819